ADVANCED PIANO SOLO

a seasoned christmas

10 CAROLS ARRANGED BY MATTHEW JANSZEN

CONTENTS	PAGE	CD TRACK
The First Noël	2	1
God Rest Ye Merry, Gentlemen	8	2
Hark! The Herald Angels Sing	13	3
It Came Upon the Midnight Clear	18	4
Jingle Bells	32	5
O Come, All Ye Faithful	23	6
O Holy Night	38	7
O Little Town of Bethleh		8
O Tannenbaum		9
Silent Night		10

ISBN 978-1-4234-8376-2

HAL•LEONARD®
CORPORATION
7777 W. BLUEMOUND RD. P.O. BOX 13819 MILWAUKEE, WI 53213

In Australia Contact:
Hal Leonard Australia Pty. Ltd.
4 Lentara Court
Cheltenham, Victoria, 3192 Australia
Email: ausadmin@halleonard.com.au

Visit Hal Leonard Online at
www.halleonard.com

THE FIRST NOËL

17th Century English Carol
Music from W. Sandys' *Christmas Carols*
Arranged by Matthew Janszen

4
4
f
8va

(8va)
mf
(8va)
8va
(8va)

ff
f
rit.
mp
Slowly, freely
mf a tempo
molto rit.
8vb

GOD REST YE MERRY, GENTLEMEN

19th Century English Carol
Arranged by Matthew Janszen

mf
mf

f
p
mp
mf poco rit.
a tempo

rit.
mp a tempo
8va

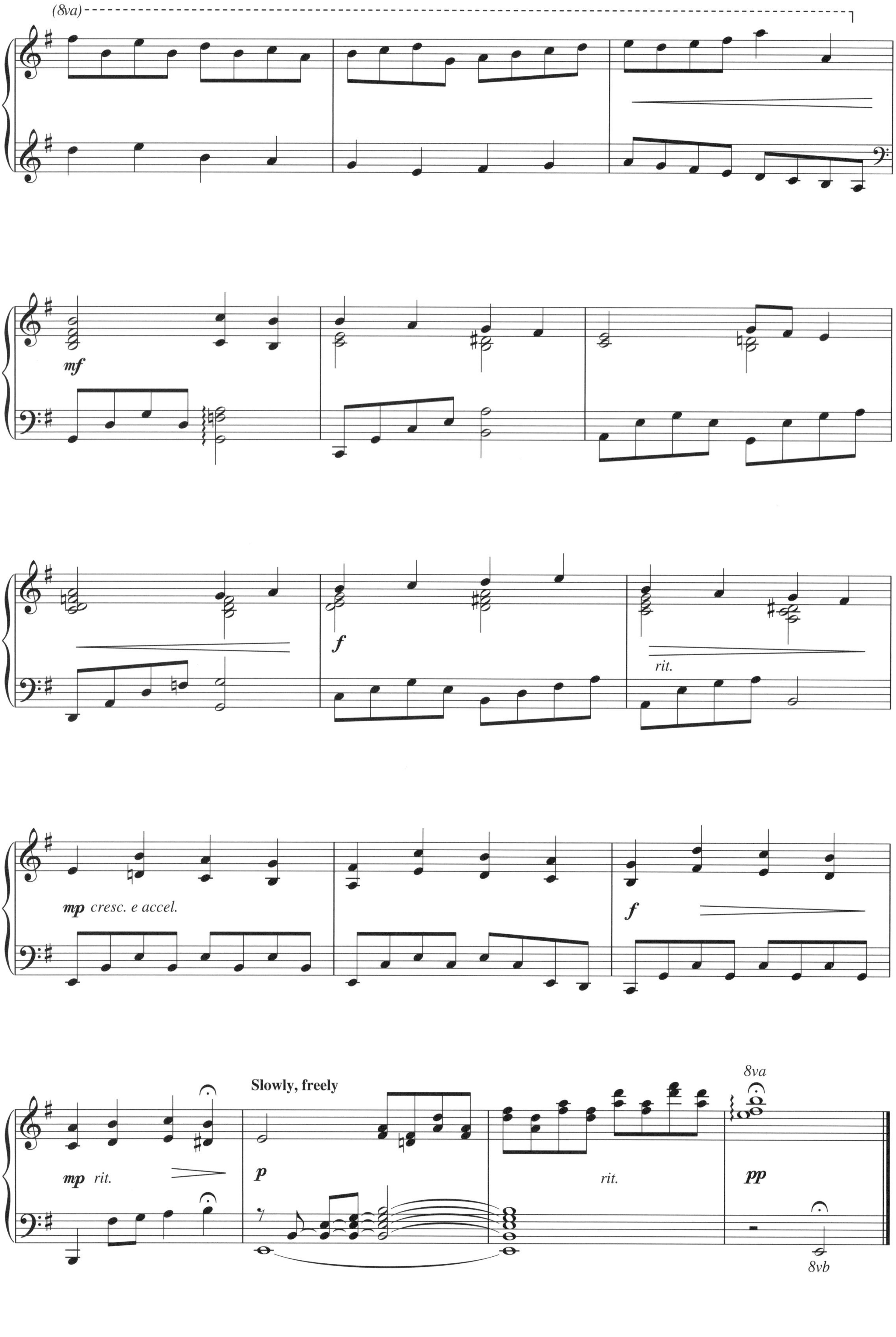
(8va)
mf
f
rit.
mp cresc. e accel.
f
Slowly, freely
mp rit.
p
rit.
8va
pp
8vb

HARK! THE HERALD ANGELS SING

Words by CHARLES WESLEY
Altered by GEORGE WHITEFIELD
Music by FELIZ MENDELSSOHN-BARTHOLDY
Arranged by Matthew Janszen

rall.
a tempo
ff

mf
f

6

6
ff
8va
8vb

IT CAME UPON THE MIDNIGHT CLEAR

Words by EDMUND HAMILTON SEARS
Music by RICHARD STORRS WILLIS
Arranged by Matthew Janszen

mf
p sub.
mf
L.H.
f

8va
8va
L.H.
L.H.
L.H.
8va
mp
mf
f
mf

f
mf
mp

O COME, ALL YE FAITHFUL

Music by JOHN FRANCIS WADE
Latin Words translated by FREDERICK OAKELEY
Arranged by Matthew Janszen

p
mf
p
mf
mp
cresc.
8va
f

(8va)
ff
(8va)
(8va)
(8va)

f
mp
mf
f

mf
f

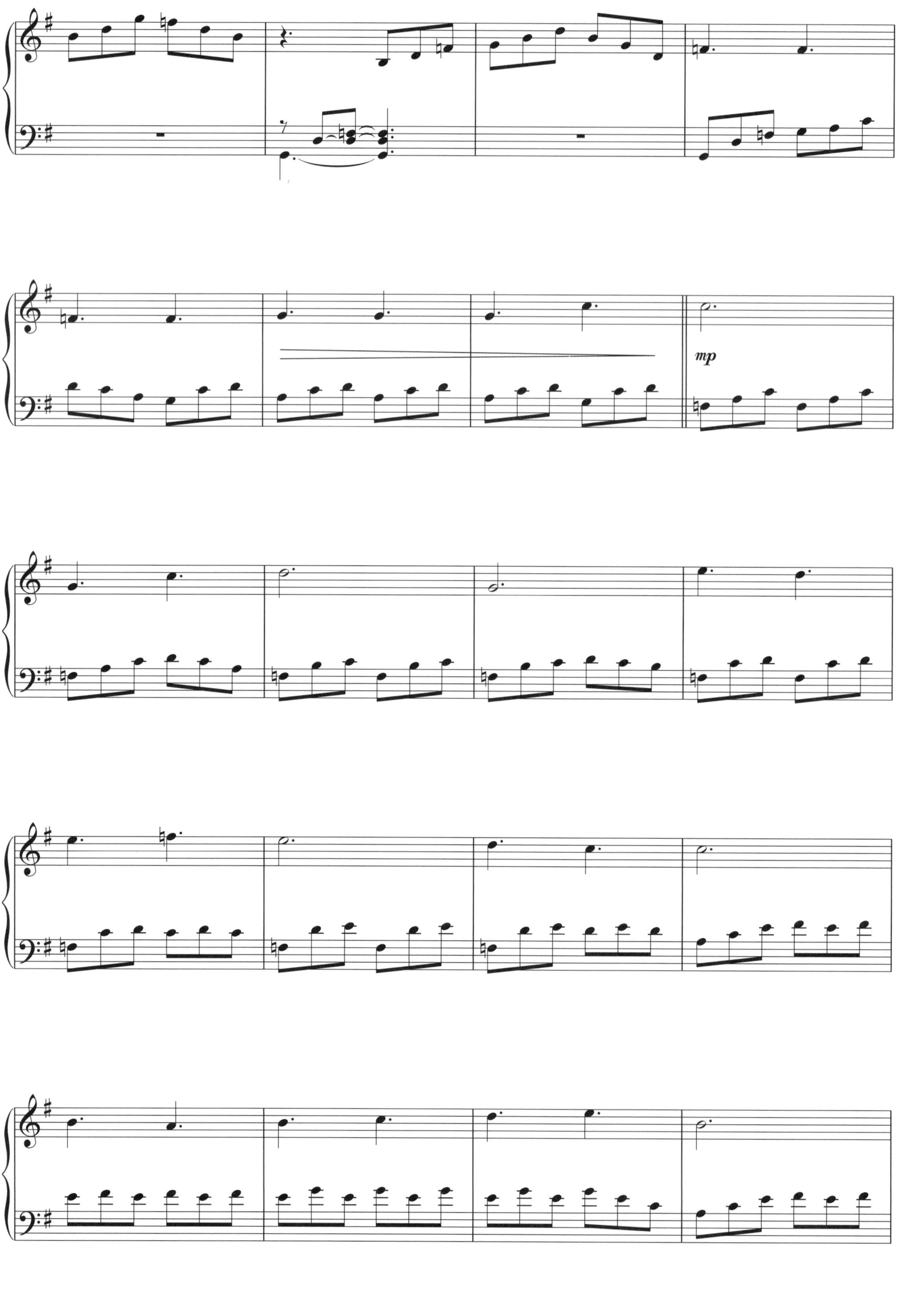
mp

mf
p
cresc.
f

L.H.
8va
R.H.
ff
mf

f
8va
(8va)
mf

JINGLE BELLS

Words and Music by J. PIERPONT
Arranged by Matthew Janszen

mf
8va
(♪ = ♪)
mp
(8va)
(8va)
mf

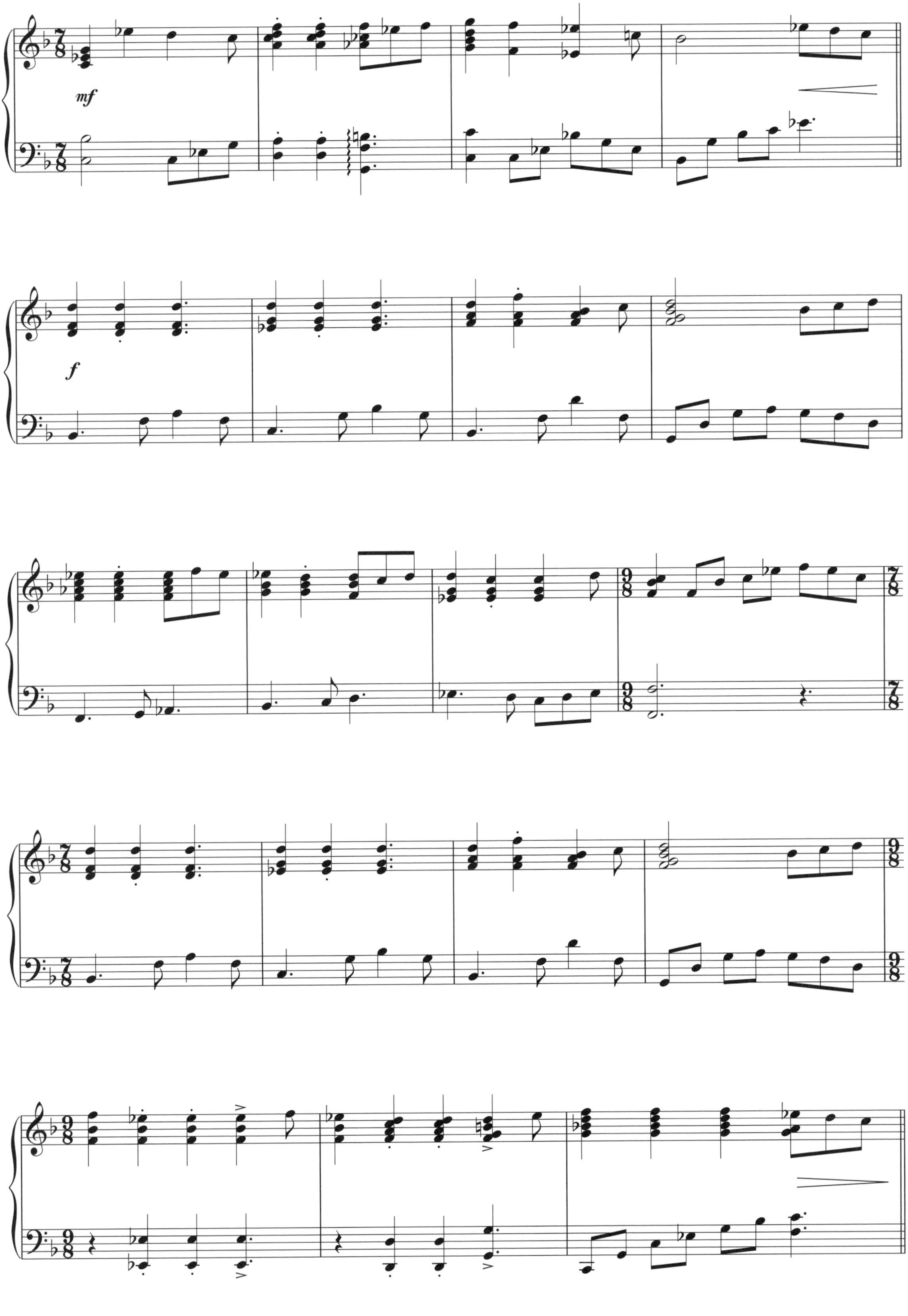
mf
f

mp
f
mf

mp
mf
f
8va
mp

O HOLY NIGHT

French Words by PLACIDE CAPPEAU
English Words by JOHN S. DWIGHT
Music by ADOLPHE ADAM
Arranged by Matthew Janszen

Slowly, with feeling (♩. = 66)

Bring out melody
p
sim.
8va
mp

mf
f

ff
f
mf
ff
rit.
a tempo
mf

8va
3
3
3
3
3
8vb
2
2
2
2
f
rit.
mp a tempo
rit.
p

O TANNENBAUM

Traditional German Carol
Arranged by Matthew Janszen

rit.
a tempo
Slightly faster
p
mp
rit.
f

a tempo
p sub.
f
ff
mf
mp
rit.
p

O LITTLE TOWN OF BETHLEHEM

Words by PHILLIPS BROOKS
Music by LEWIS H. REDNER
Arranged by Matthew Janszen

Moderately slow, freely (♩ = 88)

mp
poco rit.
mf a tempo
3
mp

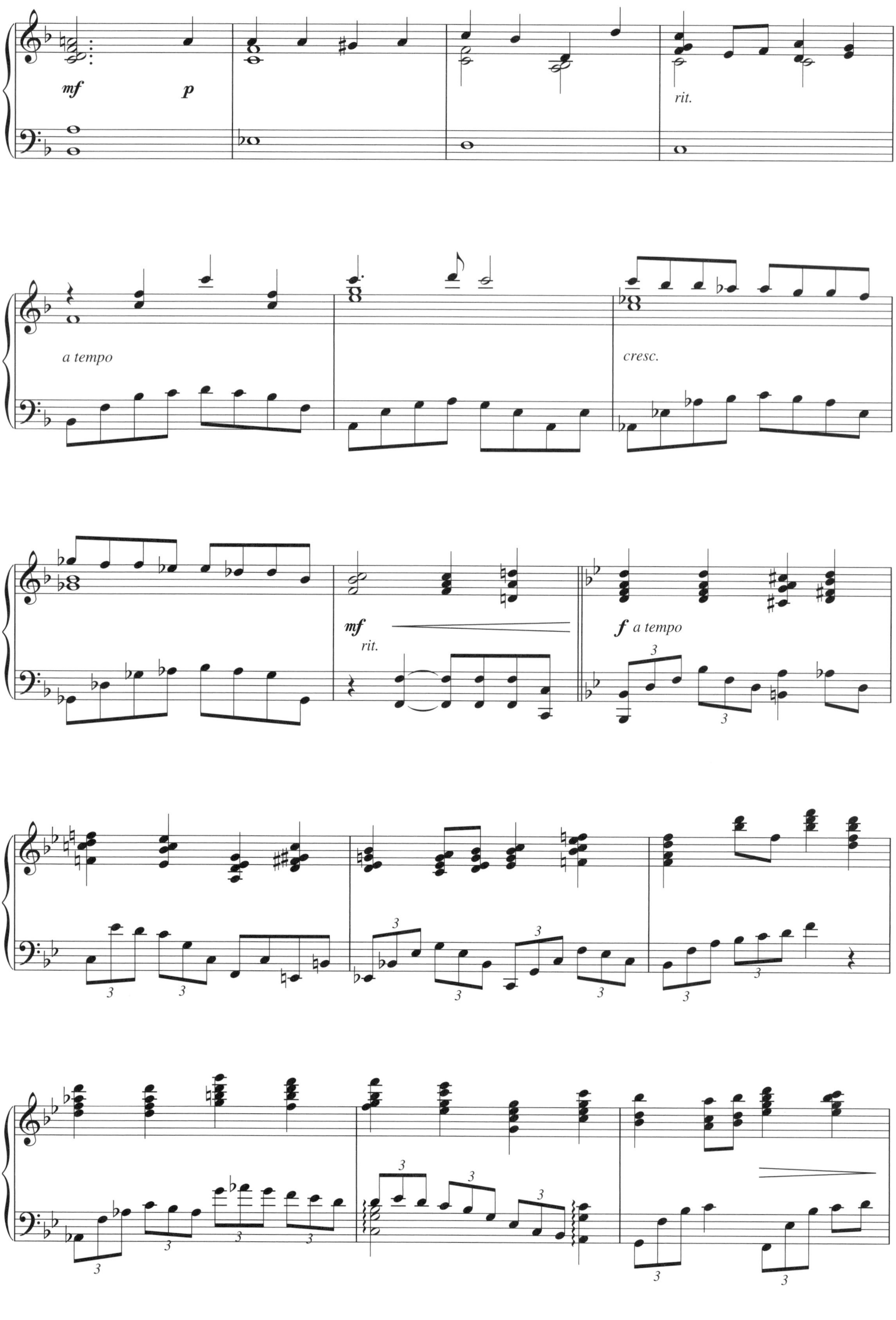
mf
p
rit.
a tempo
cresc.
mf
rit.
f a tempo

mf
mp
3
p
poco rit.
cresc., moving forward
mf
rit.
mp
p a tempo
rit.
pp

SILENT NIGHT

Words by JOSEPH MOHR
Translated by JOHN F. YOUNG
Music by FRANZ X. GRUBER
Arranged by Matthew Janszen

mp
p
mf
mp

mf
rit.
p cresc., moving forward

f
rit.
mf a tempo

f
mf
poco rit.
Slightly slower (♩ = 88)
8va
mp
(8va)
rit.
p